I0816308

NICENE CREED

I believe in one God,
the Father Almighty,
maker of heaven and earth
and of all things visible and invisible.

And in one Lord Jesus Christ,
the only-begotten Son of God,
begotten of His Father before all worlds,
God of God, Light of Light,
very God of very God,
begotten, not made,
being of one substance with the Father,
by whom all things were made;
who for us men and for our salvation came down from heaven
and was incarnate by the Holy Spirit of the virgin Mary
and was made man;
and was crucified also for us under Pontius Pilate.
He suffered and was buried.
And the third day He rose again according to the Scriptures
and ascended into heaven
and sits at the right hand of the Father.
And He will come again with glory to judge both the living and the dead,
whose kingdom will have no end.

And I believe in the Holy Spirit,
the Lord and giver of life,
who proceeds from the Father and the Son,
who with the Father and the Son together is worshiped and glorified,
who spoke by the prophets.
And I believe in one holy Christian and apostolic Church,
I acknowledge one Baptism for the remission of sins,
and I look for the resurrection of the dead
and the life ☩ of the world to come. Amen.

Copyright © 2025 Concordia Publishing House
3558 S. Jefferson Ave., St. Louis, MO 63118-3968
1-800-325-3040 • cph.org

Manufactured in China/064630/341050

1 2 3 4 5 6 7 8 9 10 34 33 32 31 30 29 28 27 26 25

THE NICENE CREED

ILLUSTRATED FOR FAMILIES

PATRICK JAMES BAYENS

ILLUSTRATED BY NICOLE CHOI

WHY WE SAY THE CREED

When we say the Nicene Creed in church, we all stand and face the altar. We do that because when we say the Creed, we are telling God what He first told us about Himself and how He loves us. Telling God what He told us says that His Word is good.

The Creed is like an adult holding my hand when I cross the street. It helps me use the Bible safely and surely. The Creed helps me speak about God as the friends of Jesus and the first Christians did.

ITS HISTORY AND SIGNIFICANCE

The Nicene Creed was written in the year 325 by over three hundred bishops who had traveled many miles to a city called Nicaea. Emperor Constantine the First had asked them to come. It was written because some didn't like what Jesus' special friends, called apostles, had taught: that the Son of God is eternal with the Father. Fifty-six years later, other bishops came to a city called Constantinople. They added words to make sure we say that the Holy Spirit is also God, with the Father and the Son, and that Jesus' "kingdom will have no end." The Creed we now use was approved by the bishops who gathered in the city of Chalcedon in the year 451. It became part of the Divine Service in the eleventh century. It is joyfully said by nearly two billion Christians every Sunday. Including me.

I believe

I believe many things.
I believe I will wake in the morning,
so I go to bed at night.
I believe in Jesus.

in one God, the Father Almighty,

I cannot see God.

Nobody can.

But I call Him “Father.”

God can do whatever He likes.

He likes me.

maker of heaven and earth
and of all things visible
and invisible.

God made everything.
God made me.
God gave me an unseen angel guard.
He tells God what I need.

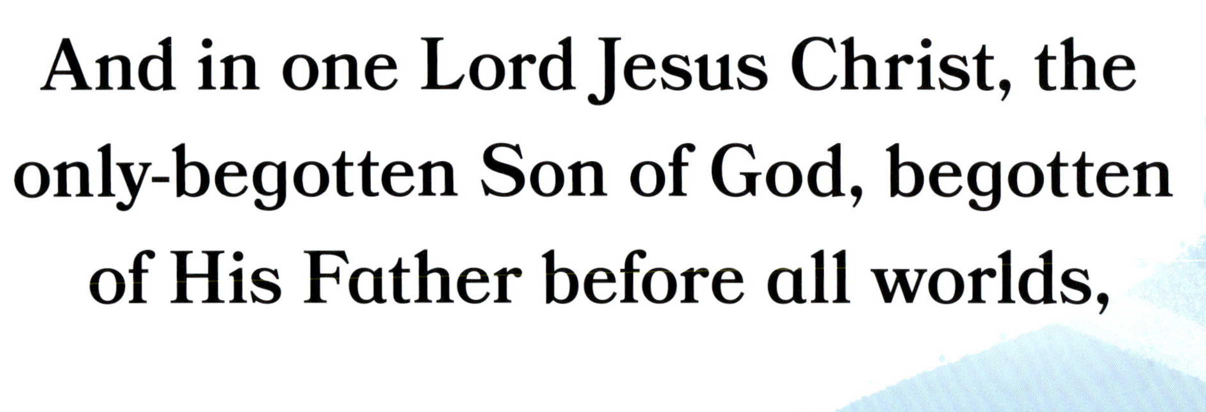

And in one Lord Jesus Christ, the only-begotten Son of God, begotten of His Father before all worlds,

Jesus is God's Son.
Always was. Always will be.
Jesus tells me about the Father,
whom I cannot see.

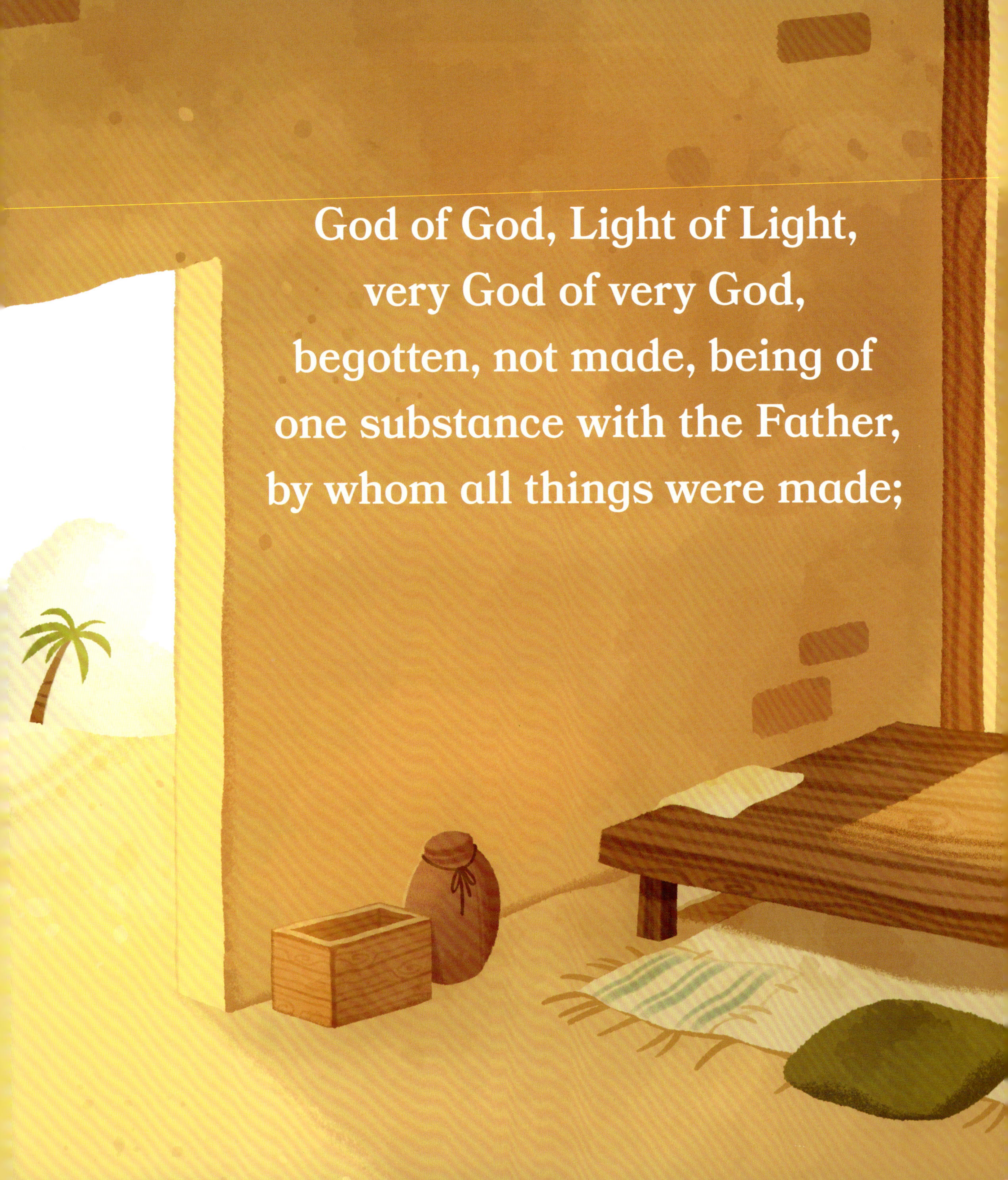

God of God, Light of Light,
very God of very God,
begotten, not made, being of
one substance with the Father,
by whom all things were made;

Jesus is God.
My Lord and my God.
Jesus is mighty like the Father.
But I can picture Jesus.

who for us men and for our salvation came down from heaven and was incarnate by the Holy Spirit of the virgin Mary

Jesus is God,
yet He was born a baby
in a very special way.
Mary is His mother.
This is Christmas for me.

and was made man;

Jesus breathed my air.
He ate. He drank. He cried.
Jesus learned to read.
He learned to sing.
He prayed. He played. He obeyed.

and was crucified
also for us under
Pontius Pilate.
He suffered and
was buried.

Jesus let Himself be arrested
and beaten badly.
He willingly died on a cross for us.
The cross means
Jesus hugs me
tight.

And the third day He rose again according to the Scriptures and ascended into heaven and sits at the right hand of the Father.

After Jesus died,
the Father made Jesus live.
Over five hundred friends saw Him.
He rules everything.
Nothing can kill Jesus now.

And He will come again with glory to judge both the living and the dead, whose kingdom will have no end.

One day Jesus will appear
in power
and make everything bad
go away.
I will live with Jesus
forever.

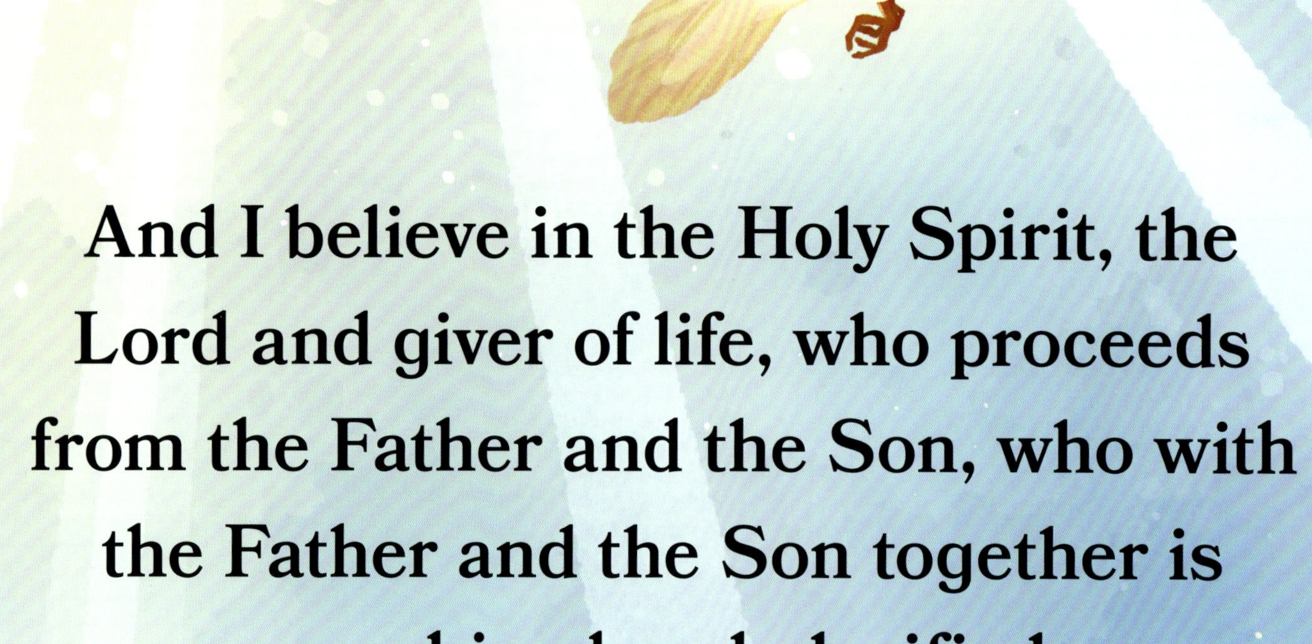

And I believe in the Holy Spirit, the Lord and giver of life, who proceeds from the Father and the Son, who with the Father and the Son together is worshiped and glorified,

The Holy Spirit is God
with the Father and the Son.
The Spirit prays for me
inside me.
I pray to Him
with Him.

who spoke by
the prophets.

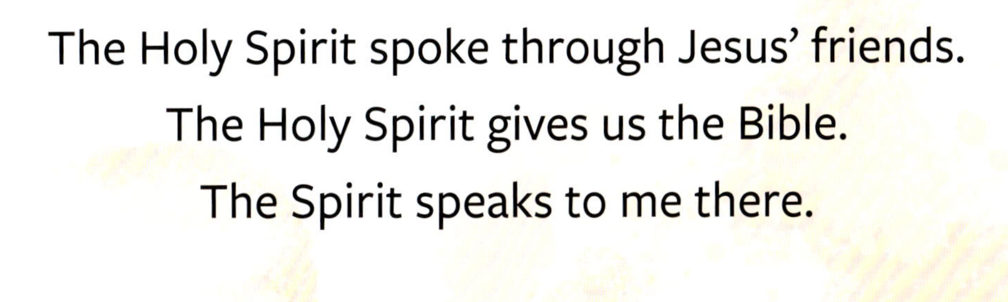

The Holy Spirit spoke through Jesus' friends.
The Holy Spirit gives us the Bible.
The Spirit speaks to me there.

And I believe in one holy Christian and apostolic Church, I acknowledge one Baptism for the remission of sins, and I look for the resurrection of the dead and the life ✠ of the world to come. Amen.

I am baptized
into God's very large family:
people here
and in heaven.
All of them are forgiven
like me.

FOR ADULTS

The text of the Nicene Creed was based on shorter and older baptismal creeds, and it was structured around 1 Corinthians 8:6 ("There is one God, the Father, from whom are all things and for whom we exist, and one Lord, Jesus Christ, through whom are all things and through whom we exist."). All the words and phrases of the Creed were drawn from Scripture, with the exception of the expression "being of one substance" (Greek: *homoousios*), or in other translations "being of the same substance" or simply "consubstantial," which was deemed necessary by the Council in order to counter the claim of one Arius. This Alexandrian pastor had been insisting that the Son was a creation of God, that He was merely a "being of like substance"—*homoiousios*—"with the Father." The 318 orthodox bishops at Nicaea rejected this teaching as unapostolic as it did not comport with the teaching of the apostolic Scriptures as a whole. The Word, who became incarnate, died, and was raised, was, and is, fully God. Ultimately, what was at stake was a sacramental issue: Into whom are we baptized? (The Father, Son, and Holy Spirit) What are we given in the Holy Supper? (The full body, blood, soul, and divinity of the exalted Christ) What do we receive in Holy Absolution? (The full forgiveness of sins secured by the death of the incarnate, eternal Word)